# Dedication

To my beautiful daughters, Sydney, Zara, and Elsie,

This book is dedicated to you with all my love. Being your mother is my greatest joy, and watching you navigate life fills my heart with pride. You inspire me daily to strive to be the best version of myself. Always remember that you have the power to achieve anything you set your mind to. Embrace the art of visualization, strategize your dreams, and witness how you create the lives you envision. Never give up; if you encounter setbacks, rise again, learn from those experiences, and keep moving forward. Your potential is limitless, and I will always be here, praying for you and eagerly anticipating the incredible paths you will forge.

# CREATE

## THE LIFE OF YOUR

# DREAMS

**WRITTEN BY BUSIE MATSIKO**

Published and Printed by Yacobu Publishing.

CREATE THE LIFE OF YOUR DREAMS

# TABLE OF CONTENTS

# INTRODUCTION

**From Wall Street to Vision Boards**—My Journey to Strategic Visualization

We all want to achieve great things in our lives. Whether it be an ambitious project, a successful relationship, college graduation, launching a new business, or building a healthy life for ourselves and our families, every single one of us has ambitious goals inside of us.

The question becomes, how do we manifest the great goals within us? Manifesting greatness is a journey and every journey requires a roadmap. It's not enough for us to desire a great life, we must know how to acquire our desire.

Creating a vision board is a creative, practical, structured, and focused approach to visualizing the great ideas, businesses, connections, growth, health, and wealth you desire.

The visualization techniques outlined in this book have been used by entrepreneurs, CEOs, students, celebrities, creatives, employees, and even full-time parents to create their dream lives and achieve great goals.

In a world driven by goals and aspirations, the importance of visualization and manifestation cannot be overstated. The power of vision is that it takes you to the end before you even begin. You get to envision your desired future before taking a single step. When you've been away from a loved one for a while and you know they are coming to see you soon; you envision what it will feel like when you see and hug them again after such a long time. The feeling of envisioning this reunion releases a new level of excitement and passion in you to anticipate their arrival. The vision board experience is the same; you envision your desired future and the excitement to take the next step to creating is released because the vision isn't real when you get there; it becomes real when you first see it in your heart and imagine it in your mind.

Vision can transcend human limitations and geographical barriers, transforming our mindset into one of boundless possibilities.

All it takes is a clear vision to unlock this extraordinary potential. Whether you are an individual seeking personal growth, a team striving for success, or an organization aiming for innovation and progress, the concept of a vision board offers a wealth of opportunities. In this book, I will show you how to use a vision board as your ultimate goal-setting tool, allowing you to create your vision and see it through to completion.

A vision board is more than a mere collection of images and words; it is a dynamic tool that enables us to define our goals, ignite our creativity, and take inspired action toward our dreams. It serves as a tangible representation of our aspirations, constantly reminding us of what we are working towards and reinforcing our unwavering belief in the vast possibilities that lie ahead. Your vision board is your roadmap to creating the life of your dreams.

About seven years ago, I became intentional about vision boards and started creating them. Two years later, this morphed into a fun annual event, where I organized and invited my friends to in-person and virtual vision board creation events as a hobby.

I recall hosting a virtual vision board event during the COVID-19 pandemic, which was viewed by over 10,000 people on Facebook. I continue to receive testimonials and feedback on the impact till today. What I started over five years ago, to inspire and encourage me to overcome procrastination, began to gain traction and inspire others too.

*"Attending the vision board workshop hosted by Busie Matsiko and her team was a transformative experience. As a career professional stepping into a new role, I found the workshop to be incredibly insightful and motivating. It provided a structured space to visualize my goals and aspirations, something that is often overlooked in the hustle of academic and professional life.*

*The exercises and guidance from Busie and her team helped me to clarify my ambitions and create a tangible representation of my future. For both students and professionals, these types of workshops are invaluable; they foster a sense of direction and purpose, empowering us to pursue our dreams with confidence and clarity*

**Randy Gomez,** *Entrepreneur, CEO & Founder*

We will embark on this journey with me explaining what manifestation is, how it works, and how having a vision (whether professional or personal) is a key part of creating the future you desire. Then, I'll go through the exact step-by-step instructions needed to make your vision of the future a reality.

Manifesting your heart's greatest desires, whether in business, relationships, or your surroundings, is completely within your power. In this book, I will show you the ins and outs of manifestation and how starting with a vision of your desired future can bring that future to life. We will explore how to manifest your dreams through the process and power of directed intention, focus, and action.

Over the past decade, I've worked with top CEOs, entrepreneurs, leaders, and visionaries around the world to employ these practices for success in business and personal life matters. Today, I share my experience and knowledge with you so that you too can manifest what you wish to see in yourself, and your reality.

Within the pages of this book, we'll embark on a journey to explore the art of manifesting vision boards. We'll delve deep into how vision boards can empower individuals, teams, and organizations to achieve greatness. We will engage practical strategies, real-life examples, and expert insights, we'll uncover the transformative impact that vision boards can have on personal, relational, and team growth. Get ready to embark on a transformative journey where your dreams and aspirations come to life.

Manifestation is real. Your ability to create the future you desire is within your reach. It all starts with a vision.

*"Faith is taking the first step, even when you don't see the whole staircase."*

*Dr. Martin Luther King, Jr.*

## Starting with a Few Definitions.

In this book, we will be using some terms that might be unfamiliar to some since we will encounter those terms several times. So, before we set off on our journey discussing the power of vision and the practical ways in which we can use it to our advantage, let's drop some definitions first.

**Manifestation:** This is the process of turning your visualized goals into reality through focused intention and action. This is why vision boards are so powerful, they help us manifest our desires and goals. We will explore this further, later.

**Law of Attraction:** The principle behind manifestation is the law of attraction, which suggests that you attract into your life whatever you focus on. By maintaining a positive and focused mindset, you draw positive outcomes towards you.

 For example, a writer who constantly envisions themselves as a published author may find themselves more inclined to write daily, network with publishers, and take necessary steps to achieve their goals. The same as any discipline, career, or goal. You must surround your mind with all the elements that support that vision.

**Intentional Action:** Manifestation isn't just about thinking positively; it requires taking deliberate steps toward your goals. Visualization sets the stage, but intentional action brings the vision to life.

For example, an entrepreneur who visualizes their business succeeding must also take concrete steps like creating a business plan, seeking investors, connecting with potential clients, and marketing their products.

## The Power of Vision

Everything you have ever seen, felt, or experienced was mentally formed in your mind before it became physically manifested.

You thought of each of your achievements before they became a reality. Vision is not accidental, it's an intentional and mental conception of your desired result before physical manifestation. That business you wanted to start? You dreamt of how it would operate, and the people it would serve. The house you wanted to buy and renovate? You saw and felt yourself standing in the living room after the building project was complete.

You saw yourself wearing your cap and gown on graduation day; despite some of the courses being challenging. Vision helps you see it, so you can live it.

Each of your achievements and the goals you reached were created in your mind before they existed in the world — that's what it means to have a vision.

Vision holds the secret to success. If you want to create anything transformational, you will need to comprehend and harness the power of vision. We'll take a deeper dive shortly to help you grasp and engage this concept accurately.

At some point, we've all visualized things we'd love to see in the future. Visualization is the creation of a mental picture of your desired future.
It could be that perfect job, the dream car, the house you'd love to buy, or the lifestyle you would lead if you had the necessary funds. Oftentimes, people call this "daydreaming," but it is much more powerful than that. The truth is if you engage these vision principles in the right way, they can take

on a life of their own to help you shift your present reality in your desired one.

**The power of vision is that it takes you to the end before you even begin.** Vision is a powerful force that propels us towards our desired outcomes before we embark on the journey. It can transcend human limitations and geographical barriers, transforming our mindset into one of endless possibilities.

Vision is the cornerstone of human aspiration and achievement. It enables individuals and organizations to imagine a future that doesn't yet exist and work towards making it a reality. This forward-thinking capability is crucial for setting goals, motivating actions, and measuring progress. All it takes is a clear vision to unlock this extraordinary potential. A vision board created with clarity and focus, with directed action behind it, becomes a manifestation of your desires.

## Direction and Focus

A well-defined vision serves as a roadmap, helping you navigate through life's complexities. It offers clarity on where you want to go and what you want to achieve, thus eliminating distractions and keeping you focused on your goals.

Think of a company with a vision to become the market leader in sustainable products. The vision is, in essence, the mission statement of the company and drives everything the company does. Focusing on its vision of sustainability in this example, the company can direct all of its efforts towards innovation in sustainability, influencing its research, production, and marketing strategies.

When a person or company is driven by a well-defined vision, focus is inevitable. Focus keeps you or your business on course and targets distractions and challenges.

With a clear-cut vision you are not distracted or confused and this helps you minimize errors or waste time. As you build momentum, you will make unbelievable progress regardless of the discipline or goal you are trying to achieve.

## Motivation and Inspiration

Vision fuels your inner drive and motivates you to take action. When you have a vivid picture of your desired future, you are more likely to stay committed and persevere through challenges.

An athlete visualizing themselves winning a championship can find the strength to push through rigorous training sessions and setbacks, driven by their vision of success.

Having a clear vision removes anxiety and worry because you are aware of where you are headed and what it demands to get it accomplished. You are also aware of the process involved that this will demand from you and the time frame to birth the specific vision you desire. This leaves you motivated to take the steps, you are inspired as you feel yourself get closer to making your vision a reality.

## Guidance for Decision-Making

With a clear vision, decision-making becomes easier. Clarity of vision leads to clarity of direction. You can evaluate opportunities and choices based on whether they align with your long-term goals.

An entrepreneur with a bold vision to create a business that would be a cornerstone of a community will make decisions that foster local engagement and support, even if it means turning down more lucrative but less aligned opportunities.

With a strong vision, decision-making becomes very transparent and easy to comprehend since you have your mission in mind. Therefore, the decisions you make to move towards that vision ultimately become a stepping stone toward a brighter future, even if they seem like difficult decisions to make. When decision-making is aligned with your vision, you unleash the power to transform your vision into reality.

Take for example that your vision is to achieve academic success at a particular age. After establishing how difficult it might be to graduate at the top of your class from your university, you can then make decisions that align with the vision, no matter how difficult they may seem. Deciding to study daily for a set number of hours from the beginning of the semester is a difficult decision and requires discipline but it will pay off in the end because it will lead to the reality of your desired vision. It is an action that gets you closer to your vision.

Similarly, if your vision is to be recognized as the Employee of the Year at your company, you'll have to make some tough but strategic decisions. For you to achieve your goal, you will need to meet and exceed your KPIs.

You may need to take extra courses, read books that will enlighten you on how to improve your work performance, and you may need to network with other leaders who have been in your position to leverage their advice. Doing all of these will enhance your vision, and take you closer to achieving it.

Remember this: a clear vision will enable you to make intelligent and informed decisions that will make you a trailblazer in whatever it is you are visualizing and prepare you for success.

## The Importance of Visualization and Manifestation

Visualization and manifestation are powerful tools for turning your vision into reality. By using these techniques, you can harness the power of your mind to achieve your goals.

**Visualization** involves creating a mental image of your desired outcome. When you visualize your goals regularly, you start to believe in their possibility, which in turn influences your actions and behaviors toward achieving them.

Visualization is like a **mental rehearsal**. Athletes often use it to prepare for competitions, imagining every detail of their performance. This practice helps build confidence and improves actual performance.

Athletes do this constantly. A gymnast visualizing their routine perfectly in their mind can improve their actual performance by mentally rehearsing each move.

Visualization encourages positive thinking. By focusing on what you want rather than what you fear, you cultivate a mindset geared towards success.

An artist visualizing their work being displayed in a renowned gallery can foster a positive mindset, encouraging them to persist through creative blocks.

## Overview of Vision Boards

Now that we've defined vision and manifestation, let's discuss how vision boards bring these concepts to life and how we can most effectively use them.

What is a vision board exactly? It is a visual tool — a board with imagery depicting your goals, wishes and aspirations — which you create for yourself using your unique creative abilities. It is a tangible representation of your goals and aspirations that serves as a visual reminder of what you want to achieve, helping you stay focused and motivated. The primary purpose of a vision board is to keep your goals in sight and to remind you daily of what you are working towards.

Ideally, your vision board is a collage of images, quotes, and affirmations that represent your goals and dreams. It can be created on a physical board or digitally.

In a world driven by goals and aspirations, the importance of visualization and manifestation cannot be overstated. Whether you are an individual seeking personal growth, a team striving for success, or an organization aiming for innovation and progress, the concept of a vision board offers a wealth of opportunities.

Within the pages of this book, we'll embark on a journey to explore the art of manifesting vision boards. We delve deep into how vision boards can empower individuals, teams, and organizations to achieve greatness.

Through the exploration of practical strategies, real-life examples, and expert insights, we uncover the transformative impact that vision boards can have on personal and collective growth. Get ready to embark on a transformative odyssey where your dreams and aspirations come to life.

## Working with a Vision Board

Creating a vision board is an exciting and creative process that helps you visualize and manifest your goals. Vision boards are a key element in manifestation. It is a tangible representation of your dreams and aspirations, using images, quotes, and symbols to inspire and motivate you.

Here, I will show you how to use a vision board in your manifestation and goal-setting work. This is a simple (but powerful!) tool that can be used by business leaders, entrepreneurs, or anyone looking to make changes to reach their goals.

In the coming chapters, we'll delve into the steps to create your vision board, from gathering materials to curating images and assembling the final product. But first, I'll provide a primer on how vision boards work in tandem with manifestation and goal-setting.

## Benefits of Using a Vision Board

You might be wondering why you would want to use a vision board to manifest your goals. Why not just write down what you want to achieve and think positively about your goal? Here are reasons why a vision board is an optimal way of harnessing the energy of your vision to achieve your goals.

- **Clarifies Your Vision.** Creating a vision board helps clarify your goals and make them more concrete. It forces you to articulate what you want in life. By selecting specific images and words for your vision board, you gain clarity on what you truly want to achieve.

- **Enhances Focus:** By visually representing your goals, a vision board enhances your focus and concentration on what matters most. A vision board can help an aspiring musician focus on their goal by reminding them daily of their commitment to practice and improve.

- **Boosts Motivation:** Seeing your goals depicted on a vision board can boost your motivation and encourage you to take action. An entrepreneur can use a vision board to stay motivated by visualizing their business's success and the steps needed to get there.

- **Encourages Persistence:** A vision board can help you stay persistent in the face of obstacles, reminding you that your dreams are worth the effort. During challenging times, a vision board can serve as a reminder of your long-term goals and the progress you've made, encouraging you to keep going.

## Daily Reminder

Placing your vision board in a prominent location ensures that you see it regularly. This constant reminder keeps your goals at the forefront of your mind. If you place your vision board near your workspace, it will remind you daily to take actions that align with your goals.

## Source of Inspiration

On days when you feel discouraged, your vision board can serve as a source of inspiration, reminding you of your dreams and the reasons why you are pursuing them. Looking at your vision board during tough times can rekindle your passion and remind you why you started your journey.

*"Don't limit your dreams, don't limit the possibilities, and keep your faith high because whatever you put down, you can achieve. You must write your vision down and make it plain. For me, seeing my vision board on top of my bed every single day, seeing exactly what I want to achieve, is inspiring. I'm so grateful to Busie for opening up that door for us to come into the room, young and old to share our experiences. Many people have been coming to these events for years and have seen their visions come to pass. It's really encouraging and inspiring."*

— **MOE,** *Award-winning musician, songwriter, and motivational speaker*

# CHAPTER ONE
# UNDERSTANDING VISION BOARDING

Understanding is the foundation for the successful application of any principle or concept. The more you understand the concept, the better you apply it. My journey with vision boarding got better and my results increased as I gained a better understanding of how it works. In this chapter; we will define vision boarding and lay the foundation for successful application.

## What is vision boarding?

A vision board is an aspirational and inspirational collage of images, pictures, and affirmations that represent and project your dreams, goals, and desires. It's a visual representation or roadmap of how you envision the life of your dreams over a period of time.

## Why Visual Goal Setting Works

*"The best way to predict your future is to create it."*
*- Abraham Lincoln*

We live in a sight and sound generation. We are inspired by what we see and having a pictorial representation of your vision keeps you inspired to chase and experience your dreams.

## Defining your vision

In Abraham Lincoln's famous quote above, he reiterates the power of vision. Visualization is strong because it creates a compelling force to drive you to birth that vision into reality by creating it.

As we've touched on already, vision is the ability to imagine and see in your mind's eye a desired future state or outcome. It goes beyond the present circumstances and helps us set goals and make decisions.

We've been trained by tradition, culture, and society to "see" things as they are; that's a limited use of your vision. Visualization helps you see things as you desire them to be not as they are.

Having a clear vision provides direction, purpose, and motivation in both your personal and professional lives.

A vision serves several functions.
It provides clarity by defining what we want to achieve and the specific outcomes we desire. It aligns our actions with our values and passions, inspiring us to overcome obstacles and think creatively. Thinking creatively produces creative results in the pursuit of your dreams.

A vision also acts as a way of measuring your progress and celebrating milestones. It allows you to evaluate your achievements and adjust our course if needed. It brings a sense of purpose and fulfillment as you see the impact of your efforts and the realization of your dreams. There is so much joy in seeing your vision manifest over time.

The process of vision begins with self-reflection and understanding our values and aspirations. Visualization practices help you create a mental picture of your desired future. Consistent affirmation and inspired action help you transform your vision into reality.

It's important to regularly evaluate and adjust your vision as you grow and evolve. Reassessing your vision helps you identify new opportunities and adapt to new challenges while maintaining the path that resonates with you.

In summary, having a vision is essential for personal and professional growth. It provides clarity, purpose, and motivation. It guides your actions and helps you achieve your goals.

Through self-reflection, visualization, and consistent action, we can manifest our vision and create the future we desire.

## Vision Board: my story

A vision board, therefore, is a tangible extension and expression of your vision. It is a powerful tool that helps bring clarity, creativity, motivation, and accountability to our goals and aspirations.

It is a visual representation of what we desire to achieve, serving as a constant reminder that we must perspire to acquire our desired dreams.

I remember my late father, James R. Matsiko Esq (God rest his soul in peace) used to emphasize the importance of writing things down to help ingrain them in the brain.

It took me a while to realize that he was right. Similarly, creating a vision board has a similar effect. It's like planting a seed in your mind and watching it grow into reality. It helps us focus on our goals and motivates us to take action. Have you ever wondered why companies spend millions on billboard advertising? They know people are inspired by what they see. What you see inspires you to act. When your vision is constantly in front of you, you keep moving forward in the direction of your vision. Seeing isn't just believing, seeing inspires you to become the version of yourself in your vision.

About seven years ago, I began to be intentional about vision boards and started writing them and this morphed into fun annual events including in-person and virtual events I organized and invited my friends to as a hobby. I recall having a virtual event during COVID-19 which was viewed by over 10,000 people on Facebook. I continue to receive testimonials and feedback on the impact of the events.

What I started over five years ago, to inspire and encourage me to overcome procrastination, began to gain traction and inspire others too. I gathered images of successful things I wanted to manifest, which included attending the World Economic Forum in Davos, Switzerland. I also included quotes and Bible verses to strengthen my faith and wrote down my desire to become an author on manifesting vision boards. This year, after seven years, I manifested both of those goals.

My vision board serves as a powerful tool that keeps me focused and reminds me of the impact I want my book to have on every reader.

Every time I look at my vision board, I feel a surge of motivation and determination to continue working on my manuscript. It served as a constant reminder that my dream of becoming a published author is within reach. You are experiencing my reality as a reader of this book.

Whether we choose to create a physical vision board using materials like a cork board and cut-out images, or a digital version using online tools or apps, the key is to choose visuals that reflect our goals and aspirations. Regularly engaging with our vision board, updating it as our dreams evolve, and sharing it with others for accountability can further enhance its effectiveness. However, when sharing your vision board with others; share with supportive people. You need people to encourage you on your journey to manifest the life of your dreams.

To sum up, a vision board is a personalized and customizable tool that helps you clarify your vision, stay motivated, and take action toward your goals.

It serves as a constant reminder of what we want to achieve and inspires us to make our dreams a reality. Unleash your creativity and create a vision board that will guide you on your journey toward success in any field you choose.

**Vision is the ability to imagine and envision a desired future state or outcome.**

Everyone should have a vision for life because it empowers you to live by design, not default. "Que Sera Sera: whatever will be, will be" is waiting for life to happen to you, not through you. Envision the life of your dream and step out to manifest it. Don't wait for life to happen to you, envision your life as it should be and go create that vision.

You can envision a perfect job while working through a challenging one, have a vision of a successful business before you embark on your entrepreneurial adventure, you can see yourself in a loving relationship despite your past experiences, and have a vision of building a harmonious family is possible by having a vision of it.

If you don't like your past experiences or your present story; it's time for a new vision. If you want to change your outlook, you have to change what and how you are looking at life. A new vision creates a new story.

Vision will help you focus on a new story and narrative instead of past failures and disappointments.

Simply stated, vision is the ability to imagine and envision a desired future state or outcome. It goes beyond the present circumstances and helps us set goals and make decisions. Having a clear vision provides direction, purpose, and motivation in both our personal and professional lives.

A vision also provides clarity by defining what we want to achieve and the specific outcomes we desire. It aligns our actions with our values and passions, inspiring us to overcome obstacles and think creatively. It brings a sense of purpose and fulfillment as we see the impact of our efforts and the realization of our dreams.

The process of vision begins with self-reflection and introspection, understanding our values and aspirations. Visualization practices help us mentally picture our desired future and experience it as if it has already happened. Consistently affirming and taking inspired action toward our vision manifests it into reality.

## Why You Should Have a Vision Board

The importance of a vision board can't be overemphasized. It is the physical, visual embodiment of your inner vision and it is what will bring it to life. A vision is like being pregnant; after a while people will start noticing your pregnancy but after about nine months; they expect to see the manifestation of your conceived vision. A Vision Board takes your "pregnancy" from conception to delivery. You can see what's within you. Visualization takes what's on the inside of you and manifests it on the outside for all to see.

**Here's how:**

- **Clarity:** Having a vision board is essential because it provides a clear path, motivates action, and helps you stay focused on your long-term goals, leading to a more fulfilling and successful life.

- **Purpose:** A vision board provides a sense of purpose, giving you life direction and meaning. It helps you understand the 'why' behind your actions and decisions.

- **Daily motivation:** As you wake up each day and the first thing you see is your vision board, it inspires your day, regardless of your mood. it reminds you of what you need to get done for the day and it leaves a tingling sensation of urgency.

- **Drives accountability:** It makes you accountable to yourself, and makes you responsible. Within a team setting, it compels everyone to achieve success as a group.

- **Ignites creativity**: Creating your vision board with precision takes skill and this will make you think in depth to create a precise and accurate vision board that captures the essence of your vision.

24

- **Magnetizes success:** The law of attraction takes place as you create your vision board because you have a clear focus of what you want, it begins to gravitate towards you.

- **Track milestones:** Your vision board becomes more fun when you start to tick out specifics from your list, like a bucket list. That exciting feeling helps you pay close attention to your goals as you aim to attain success either personally or in your office.

- **Speed:** Your vision board helps you build momentum and increase speed. When you see your dream life is within the realm of possibilities, it enhances your pace to accomplish it.

- **Inspires Hope:** Your vision board gives you hope to continue against all odds.

An environmental activist's vision might include advocating for policy changes and raising awareness about climate change, driven by a deep sense of responsibility towards the planet.

When you have a clear vision, you wake up each day with a sense of purpose. This not only enhances your motivation but also gives your life a deeper sense of fulfillment and satisfaction.

A compelling vision serves as a powerful motivator. It inspires you to work hard and persevere, even in the face of challenges and setbacks.

A medical student might stay motivated through years of rigorous study by keeping their vision of becoming a doctor and helping others at the forefront of their mind.

Motivation fueled by a clear vision is enduring. It helps you maintain enthusiasm and commitment, pushing you to keep going when the going gets tough. A vision helps you maintain focus on your long-term goals, preventing you from getting distracted by short-term temptations or obstacles.

An entrepreneur with a vision of building a successful company will stay focused on business development, even when faced with distractions or setbacks. Focus is essential in a world full of distractions. A clear vision acts as a constant reminder of your priorities, helping you allocate your time and energy more effectively.

## Why visual goal setting works

Having a vision has transformed my life. I was able to manifest many of my desires simply because I took the first step of visualizing and defining my goals. All notable people both past and present, be they world leaders, inventors, pioneers of amazing things, sports athletes, record breakers, and trailblazers — they all started with a vision. Most of them wrote out their goals and all of them took disciplined steps daily to make small movements towards reaching those goals.

Visual goal setting works. Anyone can have a vision — regardless of what your life looks like, regardless of what has happened in your past. The quality of your vision also reflects the quality of results you will get. Don't forget to always think big.

One of the dynamic things about goal setting is that it doesn't cost you anything to do but pays you everything you desire if you follow through. It doesn't require you to be successful before you set vision goals but setting vision goals increases your success possibilities.

## EVALUATE YOUR GOALS

It's important to regularly evaluate and set our goals as we grow and evolve. By reassessing our vision, we can adapt to new opportunities and challenges, staying on a path that resonates with us. Below are some other reasons why it's important to set goals by visualizing them:

- **Focus Driven:** Having visual goals gives you clarity and keeps you focused in a world where distractions are everywhere, a compelling vision keeps you bulletproof against distractions.

- **Action Driven**: A clear vision board drives you to take action, keeps you up at night to do extra work, and nudges you to put in more hours even when you should rest. You will be so driven, that you will think you have extra batteries. A clear vision propels you.

- **Meaning and Direction:** Having a vision board helps you to be very sure of your purpose, so you are not confused and moving in too many directions at once. You know exactly where you are headed and what you want to achieve.

If you can see it, you can believe it, and that makes it easy for you to plan your next steps. Visual prompts and reminders keep your goals at the top of your mind.

- **Staying Power to Endure Challenges:** Life is never fair to be truthful, however, you must tell yourself that you will face the challenge and win. You must be mentally tough and refuse to take no. Being clear on your visual goals gives you staying power to remain resilient when facing challenges. I remember days I would be tired and want to quit, but I then remind myself why I started.

  A compelling vision board keeps you strong regardless of the resistance that may occur.

- **Personal and Career Growth:** A strong visual goal or vision board will spur you to grow personally and in your career. It's something that you cannot hide away because your vision is always there for you to see and will compel and drive you with a strong sense of urgency.

- **Hones your Decision-Making Skills:** Setting strong vision goals will hone your decision-making skills because it will hone your focus and direction toward your vision. It will guide you to only do things that will help you attain your goal. For example, if you are an athlete aiming to be the fastest person on earth, over time your athletic skills will improve because you will make decisions to achieve that specific vision, such as practicing timed runs daily or hiring a coach.

- **Purpose-driven:** A strong visual board gives you a clear purpose of where you are headed, what you are doing, and all about. Having a meaningful life is what a well-defined vision will give you.

- **Legacy Driven**: With your visual goal well drafted, you will live a life that will add value to others. Your footprints will be remembered on the sands of time. Your vision will impact the lives of others by achieving feats worth celebrating.

*"A vision board is a concrete manifestation of our dreams and ambitions, comprising images, words, and phrases that vividly convey our desires and objectives. It acts as a potent tool that utilizes the power of visualization — a technique supported by psychological studies — to assist individuals in reaching their goals."*

— ***Davidson Toussaint,*** *Serial Entrepreneur, Visionary Chief Creative Officer*

I always love to strike a balance, so let's quickly talk about possible scenarios where sometimes visual goal setting doesn't work, and the reasons why it's not working. When people do not adhere to the principles behind using vision boards, the results won't be the same as those who methodically follow the rules.

## When Visual Goal Setting Does NOT Work: Pitfalls to Watch Out For

### Inaction

In my experience, 80% of people who fail with vision boarding are due to them not taking action. When you don't take the steps that will bring your goals to life, then it's just wishful thinking. You can look at your vision board all day, but if you don't put in the work, nothing will change. You must have a plan, you must know your next step.

Your visual goals are only as powerful as the effort you put behind them. Visualization alone will not replace the important power of visualization *and* directed hard work. So make up your mind to get the work done and hold yourself accountable.

## Disorganized goals

One of the pitfalls many people encounter is not organizing their goals, which can lead to a lack of focus and direction. Your goals should not be cumbersome and all over the place. Ensure you articulate your goals such that once anyone sees your vision board they know exactly what you are doing. If you overload your vision board with too many goals, it can be overwhelming and confusing. You don't want to exhaust your mental energy and still make zero progress.

Your visual goals only work when you stay organized and focus on prioritizing a few goals at a time. When you have mastered them and built strong discipline, then you can add goals and take more giant strides.

There is a proverb that says, "You can't chase three rabbits at once and expect to catch them all." This also applies to success in achieving your goals. Choose a few strategic KPIs at any given time and crush those milestones before you go for more so that you don't spread yourself too thin.

## Unrealistic Goals

Your visual goals must be very realistic and achievable. Focusing on unrealistic goals can set you up for disappointment. You need to set goals that challenge you but are still achievable.

For instance, it would be unrealistic for a corn farmer to have a vision board goal of tripling the corn harvest within 60 days. This goal is unrealistic because it would require perfect weather, significant changes in farming methods, extra resources, and possibly a miracle, all within a very short timeframe. The natural growth cycle for corn typically lasts 90-120 days, along with the many factors involved in farming, making this goal rather implausible. A better goal would be to simply visualize a bountiful harvest occurring in an appropriate timeframe. Of course, elements such as weather and climate are unpredictable variables, but the hard work necessary to produce a plentiful harvest is within the farmer's control.

Just like the farmer, your own goal should be ambitious, yet realistic in what you're able to accomplish. Also, pay attention to timing: vision boards don't happen overnight so your time frames must be realistic. If you're not patient, you'll burn out or give up too soon.

## Strategic and Emotional Alignment

You cannot desire to be an Oscar winner but dedicate your time to playing football. If your goals don't truly resonate with you, you won't feel motivated to achieve them. Visual goals need to have personal meaning and be strategically aligned with where you see yourself, or they'll lose their power.

When it means the world to you, that's the only thing you will focus on and nothing will be able to distract you. You must commit 100% to your goals and take the steps that will support them becoming a reality.

If your goals don't ignite a strong sense of urgency and drive, then you will not be emotionally and strategically aligned whenever you see your vision board, so it won't work the way it is intended to.

31

If you don't feel emotionally connected to your dreams; you need to take some time to reflect on your dreams. Imagine, a student studying to become a Medical Doctor just because everyone in their family is one but they want to do is be a dance instructor. It's a transferred dream on a vision board, not an inspired goal. The drive to become a Doctor advises you to take some time for introspection to figure out what you connect with emotionally and how you can make that into a visualized goal for yourself.

## Lack of Nurturing Culture

The beginning of every year is popular for the new's resolution experience. On the first day of January, millions of people set goals they desire to achieve and give up as quickly as they start a new year. For some is losing a few pounds or gaining a few healthy pounds while others aspire to buy a new house, travel the world, get hitched, or ditch an unhealthy relationship.

The months fly by and comes the end of the year and another new year on the horizon but desires are still in the dream form. Dreams aren't automatically fulfilled they are made to happen. Just like a plant you ignore, if you don't visit your visual goals often, nurture your dream board, and take the steps needed to grow it, it will eventually lose its effectiveness.
You need to review your goals regularly to stay aligned and update them as your life evolves. If you don't nurture your vision board, you will not evolve.

## Bending to Life's Pressure

Countless times I have had difficult days that gave me enough reason to leave my goals, but I know that a calm sea does not make a good sailor, you must be mentally tough and focused. Life gets in the way.

External pressures, responsibilities, or distractions can pull you away from your visual goals. If you're not disciplined, your focus will waver.

Vision boards are powerful, but they can't stop life's realities from impeding progress on your journey to achieving your set goals. You need determination to overcome distractions because they will come. If you are prepared to get to your destination, you'll be able to stay on track with your goals regardless of bumps in the road.

**In summary**
In summary, visual goal setting is essential for personal and professional growth. It provides clarity, purpose, and motivation, guiding our actions and helping us achieve our goals. Through self-reflection, visualization, and consistent action, we can manifest our vision and create the future we desire.

For your visual goals to work, you must create a vivid, emotional connection to your dreams and — importantly — take action! Visuals are a tool to keep you focused and motivated, but they're not a shortcut. You must commit to doing the real work, the hard work, and the resilience needed — no amount of visualization by itself will get you there. You can't just see your goals, you have to work for them. Surround yourself with positive energy, rack up your small wins, and give yourself a pat on the back as you make little progress. It's your unique vision, so don't let anyone or anything distract you.

# CHAPTER TWO
# DIVERSITY OF VISION BOARDS

*If you are working on something exciting that you really care about, you don't have to be pushed, The vision pulls you. - Steve Jobs*

I have a unique perspective on Vision Boarding. If you desire to sail from Toronto to New York City. Toronto is your starting point, the beginning of your dream and New York City is your destination; the manifestation of your dreams. Vision Board is your mode of transportation from your location to your destination. You now have to choose the mode of sailing. Regardless of the mode of water transportation you choose; your destination remains the same.

## Busie's Boat

There are different shades of vision boarding. When you think about different means of transportation on water, you will need to understand the core function and then specifically use it for that function, for example, a submarine is different from a raft, and a canoe is different from a yacht, but they can all help you move on water from Toronto to New York City but with different levels of speed, experience, safety, visibility, capacity, and comfort, but they eventually get you to your desired destination.

Nonetheless, while all vision boards are designed to get you to your dream destination; I will share other perspectives, origins, and diversities of vision boards so you understand their longevity, efficacy, and authority.

34

My key focus will still be what has worked for me and that is exactly what will work for you.

Welcome to Busie's Boat and thanks for using us as your transportation of choice to your dream destination.

Let's explore perspectives to broaden your knowledge then focus on what's working for me.

## Origins of Vision Boarding

Everything has a beginning, before exploring diverse perspectives on vision boarding, let's examine its origins.

The idea of a vision board dates back centuries and has been linked to various practices across cultures, primarily due to its strong association with goal-setting and visualization.

Over time, people discovered the transformative power of creating a tangible representation of their aspirations, largely because of vision boarding's consistent track record of helping individuals manifest their dreams.

## Ancient Egypt's Perspective

Vision boarding as a practice also found roots in Ancient Egypt, where goal-setting and visualization were integrated into societal rituals, artworks, and personal ambition. These practices reveal a longstanding history of using imagery and intention to shape one's life and community.

## The Earliest Use of the phrase 'Vision Board'

Our research suggests that one of the earliest uses of the phrase 'vision board' itself was in the United Kingdom, where it appeared in city planning contexts. Council leader Kevin Stephens noted, "We have had over 2,500 suggestions from the public on how to improve their city." This public feedback and goal visualization became a practical form of vision boarding, allowing for a communal and actionable approach to city development. If you want to take that a step further; architectural designs and digital models are visualizations of your dream home, school, office complex, or whatever you desire to be. Have you ever seen your kitchen remodeling project on a piece of paper or computer modeling before actually cooking in it; that's vision boarding.

## Vision Boarding and the Holy Bible

Vision boards hold spiritual significance for many. I believe vision boarding is Biblical, serving as a compass that aligns with my Christian faith. Vision boarding principles are echoed in scriptures, showing how visualization has been practiced for centuries. This connection resonates particularly with the Israelites, who used visions as divine guidance on their pioneering journeys. Here are some scriptures that reflect this practice:

- **Habakkuk 2:2** – "And the LORD answered me: "Write the vision; make it plain on tablets, so he may run who reads it."
- **Joshua 1:8** – "This Book of the Law shall not depart from your mouth, but you shall meditate in it day and night, that you may observe to do according to all that is written in it."

36

- **Proverbs 29:18** – "Where there is no vision, the people perish: but he that keepeth the law, happy is he."

## A Note on Manifestation and Religious Faith

For many, the intersection of manifestation and faith is significant. Manifesting and using vision boards can coexist with religious beliefs. Many faithful individuals, regardless of their religion, use manifestation to align with divine guidance.

As one Christian attendee of my vision board events shared, "Write the vision; make it plain on tablets, so he may run who reads it. For still, the vision awaits its appointed time; it hastens to the end—it will not lie. If it seems slow, wait for it; it will surely come; it will not delay." (Habakkuk 2:2)

With this perspective, building vision boards grounded in faith becomes a powerful experience. By writing our visions down, we can witness our goals and dreams come to life, leading to moments of gratitude and reflection on divine guidance. The other fascinating part of that passage is "so he may **run**...."

A written vision keeps you running towards accomplishing it. The more you read your vision board; the faster you run.

## The Science Behind Vision Boards: The Brain's Response to Visualization

Science shows that visualizing goals helps the brain perceive them as achievable. This isn't mystical but rather engages the brain's motivation system, making goals seem more real. Vision boards work through a psychological principle called

37

"priming," where seeing images related to aspirations enhances focus on relevant opportunities.

When you visualize your goals daily, your brain registers them as priorities, helping you notice available resources and attract people aligned with your ambitions.

## Making Vision Boards Accessible and Inclusive

Contrary to the notion that vision boards are only for those with New Age beliefs, vision boards are practical tools for setting and achieving goals. They're not about invoking a higher power but about engaging the brain in ways that naturally support motivation and resilience. Whether you're adding Bible verses, motivational quotes, or career aspirations, vision boards can be a blank canvas to reflect whatever is meaningful to you.

### Daily Motivation Through Vision Boards

Incorporate your vision board into your daily life with strategies like:

- **Daily Reflection** – Review your board each morning to reinforce commitment.
- **Daily Affirmation** – Speak positively to yourself about your dreams daily.
- **Goal Breakdown** – Divide large goals into smaller steps for achievable progress.
- **Celebrate Milestones** – Acknowledge and celebrate incremental successes.

### Embracing the Power of Intention and Visualization

38

Vision boards are accessible, engaging our minds in ways that motivate and empower us. They leverage the brain's natural inclination for visuals, aligning us with our goals.

As you continue on this amazing journey to create the life of your dreams; be inspired by the fact that vision boarding gives you a roadmap with clarity, intentionality, and consistently striving for improvement, providing a flexible, inclusive method to visualize success and stay motivated in the journey toward our aspirations.

# CHAPTER THREE
# BEYOND WISHFUL THINKING

*"Vision without action is merely a dream. Action without vision just passes the time. Vision with action can change the world."— Joel A. Barker*

Vision Board manifestation isn't magical; it's planning + seeing + action.

A vision board filled with beautiful pictures can spark inspiration, but to turn those images into reality, you must move beyond wishful thinking into practical action. Setting clear intentions and surrounding ourselves with powerful imagery can be transformative, especially when paired with actionable plans.

We can't underestimate the power of writing things down. When you commit something to paper, it's no longer just an idea; it becomes a declaration, a blueprint that you can reference and build upon. For many, writing down a vision makes it more tangible and harder to forget.

*"Inaction will keep you stagnant, but taking purposeful action leads to success. You need that first step—show up!"*
*- Busie Matsiko*

Imagery can fuel this process. When I see a picture of a place I dream of visiting, like Santorini or the Amalfi Coast, it's more than just a "pretty picture"—it's a reminder of my goals and the lifestyle I desire to achieve. The imagery motivates me to explore the practical steps needed to make it happen, from budgeting to finding and leveraging additional sources of income.

This also applies to bigger aspirations, such as financial freedom and the capacity to enjoy a "soft life." Visualizing these goals energizes me to create concrete actions that support both my dreams and my journey toward wealth. It works for me and I believe you will experience yours too.

The combination of writing and using pictures is a powerful tool for dream manifestation. Writing your desires down has true power and adding pictures, especially for visual people brings it to life and can serve as a powerful motivator that encourages you to accomplish the goals that those pictures represent.

Every movie you've ever watched was first written into a script. Movies are words in motion and action.

The principle of writing dreams and visions down is rooted in faith: the Biblical verse Habakkuk 2:2 reminds us, **"Write the vision; make it plain."** When you put a goal in writing, you create a visible reminder of your purpose. Writing down your dreams is like casting a vision that continuously pulls you closer, encouraging you to surround yourself with resources and people who align with that vision.

## BIRDS OF THE SAME FEATHER

The old English proverb; "Birds of a feather flock together" when applied to people simply means; to surround yourself with people who have similar interests, dreams, and aspirations as you. If you are surrounded by people who have negative things to say about your dream board; it will eventually get to you and slow you down.

The people we choose to connect with are as important as our dreams because they play a significant role in helping us achieve them or stopping us from achieving them. If we align ourselves with individuals who are wise, driven, or financially successful, their influence often rubs off on us, naturally elevating our journey. As the African proverb says, "If you want to go fast, go alone. If you want to go far, go together." This resonates deeply as a reminder to build a network of like-minded people who share in our aspirations.

This isn't just about attracting wealth or success but creating an ecosystem that we can rely on—a community that offers encouragement, inspiration, and sometimes even tough love.

When we nurture our relationships and build strong networks, we empower each other. It's about creating a circle where our successes contribute to each other's growth, fostering a sense of shared strength. Just as pretty images inspire us, a supportive circle of friends, colleagues, and relatives drives us toward our dreams.

This chapter is a reminder: do not underestimate the power of the positive images you choose to represent your dreams, the power of the words you use to express them, and the people you choose to surround yourself with as you continue on the journey to build the life of your dreams.

When you have accomplished a vision, congratulate yourself on manifesting that desire! However, manifesting isn't the endpoint. After reaching one of your goals, it is important to recast or redefine your vision to ensure continued growth and progress. When you accomplish a goal; it gives you momentum; maximize the momentum to cast a new vision. This will enhance your continued growth and success.

Recasting the vision for individuals, teams, and organizations involves redefining and realigning their goals, aspirations, and purposes. It requires a thoughtful and strategic approach to create a clear and compelling vision that inspires and motivates.

*"Think it through: Picture each step in your mind and take action."-Busie Matsiko*

For individuals, recasting the vision involves reflecting on personal values, strengths, and passions. It means envisioning the future they want to create for themselves, defining their goals and aspirations, and aligning their actions with their vision.

For teams, recasting the vision involves bringing together a diverse group of individuals with different skills and perspectives. It requires defining a shared purpose, setting collective goals, and fostering a collaborative and inclusive environment where everyone feels engaged, heard, and motivated to work towards a common vision.

For organizations, recasting the vision involves revisiting and redefining the company's mission, values, and strategic objectives. It requires aligning the vision with the changing needs of the market, customers, and stakeholders, and creating a roadmap for achieving long-term success.

Overall, recasting the vision is an ongoing process that requires continuous evaluation, adaptation, and communication. It helps individuals, teams, and organizations stay focused, inspired, and resilient in the face of challenges and changes.

Celebrating milestones is a crucial aspect of the journey toward achieving your goals. Recognizing and rewarding your progress, no matter how small helps maintain momentum and reinforces positive behaviors.

## Keys to Recasting Your Vision

**1. Reflect on your achievements:** Take the time to reflect on the goals you have successfully achieved. Celebrate your achievements and acknowledge the progress you have made. Reflecting on achievement increases your momentum and assures you that more is possible.

**2. Assess the current state:** Evaluate the current state of your organization, team, or personal situation. Consider the changes that have occurred, the new opportunities on the horizon, and any challenges that need to be addressed.

**3. Identify new goals and aspirations:** Think about what you want to achieve next. Consider your long-term vision and what you want to accomplish in the future. Identify new goals and aspirations that align with your values and purpose.

**4. Seek feedback and input:** Engage with stakeholders, team members, relatives, or mentors to gather their perspectives and insights. Seek feedback on the direction you are considering and gather input on potential opportunities or challenges that should be taken into account.

**5. Develop a revised vision:** Based on your reflections, assessment, and feedback, develop a revised vision

CREATE THE LIFE OF YOUR DREAMS

statement. This statement should articulate the new direction, goals, and aspirations you have identified. It should inspire and motivate others to join you in pursuing these new objectives.

**6. Communicate the revised vision:** Share the revised vision with your team, organization, or relevant stakeholders. Communicate the new goals and aspirations, and explain the reasons behind the revision. Engage others in the vision by highlighting how they can contribute and the benefits they can expect from the revised direction.

**7. Align strategies and actions:**

It's essential to align your strategies, plans, and actions with the revised vision. Ensure that your goals, initiatives, and day-to-day activities are in line with the new direction. Regularly assess progress and make any necessary adjustments to stay on track.

Recasting a vision after accomplishing the initial vision allows for continued growth, adaptation, and innovation. It keeps you motivated, focused, and prepared for new opportunities and challenges that may arise.

*"Having been a guest at one of her vision workshops and knowing Busie Matsiko for a decade-plus, she isn't just a passionate visionary, she backs up that vision by giving others the tool kit and inspiration to not just manifest but actualize dreams of their own."*

— Melissa Gonzalez, Principal, MG2, and Founder of The Lionesque Grou

45

# CHAPTER FOUR
# MINDSET PREP

*"Your past is a place to learn from, not a place to live." —*
*Tony Robbins*

Everything rises and falls on your mindset. Your mind is the central processing hub for creating the life of your dream. A strong, positive, and healthy mindset enhances your dream board's creativity. Preparing your mind for this new journey begins with reflection, and there's no better place to start than by looking back at where you've been. Too often, we set out on new paths without evaluating what's worked, what hasn't, and what lessons to take into the future from our past.

This chapter is dedicated to "the audit"—a process of honestly assessing your last year. Think of it as taking inventory, clearing mental clutter, and ultimately, preparing yourself to build something fresh and resilient. As you embark on this reflective audit; don't get stuck in what didn't work, instead focus on why it didn't work and learn from it. It's not a trip back to "Regretville"; it's an opportunity to glean from the past as you lean forward into the future.

Auditing your past year requires more than just recalling your wins and losses; it's about understanding your growth patterns, challenges, and breakthroughs. When you assess these elements objectively, you create a strong foundation for future goals. You can see where your actions align with your vision, and where you might have gotten sidetracked or missed an opportunity by not taking prompt and decisive steps.

Your goal setting needs a clear, healthy, and confident mindset, and that begins with facing what's already happened, learning from it, and, if needed, forgiving yourself for missed opportunities.

## STEPS TO CULTIVATING THE RIGHT MINDSET

### Step 1: Reflecting on Successes and Setbacks

Grab a notebook or your phone and let's start with your successes. What did you accomplish last year that you're proud of?

Go beyond the big wins and include the small, consistent steps you took that eventually led to your progress. Small wins are often overlooked but they reinforce good habits and build momentum.

Write down each win, and capture each personal victory, no matter how minor. Reflecting on these moments doesn't just boost confidence; it provides proof that you are capable of meeting goals, no matter the size.

Now, shift your attention to the setbacks. Don't look at these moments with self-criticism or judgment. This audit isn't about regret—it's about recognition. Identify areas where you fell short, the goals that may have been left incomplete, and the obstacles you faced. Ask yourself if there were recurring patterns, such as procrastination or self-doubt, that held you back. Did you have unexpected negative external factors?

Remember, the goal here is not to dwell on failure but to recognize it, understand it, and make peace with it as you extract lessons learned to avoid it in the future. Every successful journey includes bumps and detours, and each one offers valuable lessons if you're willing to look.

## Step 2: Identify Patterns and Triggers

Your next task is to identify any patterns that have emerged over the past year. Patterns are habits in disguise, and they can be either productive or counterproductive. Start by examining your daily routines, your social interactions, your work habits, and even your self-talk. For example, do you tend to lose motivation after initial excitement? Do you get overwhelmed and give up when things get tough? By identifying these tendencies, you can start making conscious adjustments that support a more constructive mindset.

Alongside patterns, consider any triggers—both positive and negative—that have impacted your progress. What kinds of events, environments, or people motivated you? Conversely, what situations or people have tended to drain your energy or dampen your enthusiasm? Acknowledging these factors will help you plan around them in the future, amplifying your strengths and avoiding pitfalls.

## Step 3: Releasing Mental and Emotional Clutter

As you reflect on the past year, it's natural for unresolved emotions to surface. Some might be positive, like pride or satisfaction, while others could be lingering frustrations, regrets, or doubts. Holding on to emotional baggage from last year's experiences can weigh you down and limit your capacity to move forward. Take some time to consciously release any negativity associated with unmet goals or setbacks. This might involve forgiveness—of yourself or others—or simply a commitment to let go of unrealistic expectations.

Consider practicing mindfulness or journaling as a way to process these emotions. When you put feelings into words, you bring them to light, allowing yourself to see them objectively and detach from them. Preparing your mind means creating space for new possibilities by letting go of what no longer serves you. If it doesn't serve you, it doesn't deserve space in your mind.

## Step 4: Setting a Mindful Intention for the Year Ahead

Once you've completed your audit, take a deep breath and focus on what lies ahead. Setting an intention for the new year is like setting a guiding star—it doesn't dictate every step, but it gives you a sense of direction and purpose. An intention could be as simple as "embrace growth" or "welcome challenges." The key is to keep it authentic and aligned with what you truly desire.

A mindful intention is more than a goal; it's a commitment to a way of life and your emotional well-being. While goals are specific targets, intentions are about the attitude and energy you bring to every moment. They serve as your mental compass, reminding you to stay connected to your journey's deeper purpose. As you prepare your mind, remember that every new goal, vision, or resolution you set will be empowered by the clarity, awareness, and balance you create in this place of reflection.

## Celebrating Milestones

Celebrating milestones along your journey is essential for maintaining motivation and reinforcing positive habits.

Recognizing even small wins can help sustain momentum and encourage a growth mindset.

Celebration can vary from personal rewards to team acknowledgments, such as sharing success stories or organizing events that honor individual and group achievements. Regularly revisiting and appreciating progress keeps the journey toward your goals rewarding and meaningful.

# CHAPTER FIVE
# GATHERING YOUR MATERIALS

"The right tools set you up for success and help you achieve great results"- Busie Matsiko

Whether you are creating your very first vision board or the first one following the strategies in this book; I'm excited to see what you create. Let's get practical. Your vision board is your focused trajectory to your goal.

This also means the materials you will need to guide you there must align with your specific goal. You must intentionally gather applicable inspirational and aspirational pictures, supplies, and other elements to create an effective dream board.

For example, If I say I want to be one of the greatest musicians of all time, I need to see myself holding a Grammy award and not an Olympic gold medal. I know winning an Olympic gold medal is great but it has nothing to do with my vision board. One of the mistakes people make is they use the wrong materials for their vision board and desire to see results in their focused vision. The wrong image inspires the wrong results. You need the right image to inspire you in the right direction to arrive at the right destination.

We've discussed what a vision is and how having a clear, focused vision is essential to achieving your desires and goals. A vision board takes that a step further by becoming a tangible representation of your vision.

Creating a vision board is a powerful technique that can help you bring your dreams and goals into reality. Here are some fundamental steps to help you create a great vision board:

## 1. Set clear intentions:

Before creating your vision board, take some time to reflect on your goals and desires. What do you want to manifest in your life? Be specific and clear about what you want to achieve. Remember to look at your vision as having already been achieved at some point in your future. You are starting with seeing the end from the beginning. Don't use "I want..." statements in your vision board, but rather, use "I have..." or "I am..." statements. Your subconscious mind needs to understand that what you want has already happened. This is what manifestation is all about. It's like your dream vacation to Hawaii has already happened; you are just on a journey to discover how you got there.

## 2. Gather supplies:

Get a poster board or cardboard, magazines, scissors, glue, markers, and any other materials you want to use for your vision board. You can also use digital tools to create a virtual vision board.

You can get newspapers and magazines at a shop, or even for free at yard sales. Local supermarkets carry coupon books, real estate papers, and other free magazines that can inspire your vision board. Thrift stores often carry vintage magazines and books that can add an element of design and character to your vision board.

If you're taking a digital approach, websites like Pinterest, Unsplash, and Shutterstock have a vast array of printable images — just remember to double-check the licensing requirements for any visuals you want to use.

Don't hesitate to reach out to family, friends, and colleagues to see if they have any magazines or printed material that could be a source of inspiration. Each of these avenues can contribute to valuable visuals that will bring your vision board to life!

I discovered when faced with a limited supply of physical magazines or newspapers, you can use search engines like Google or social media platforms like Pinterest for ideas. You can search for symbols of wealth, wellness, or vacations like look for pictures of money, healthy food, or nice places in Cape Town among others. You can also add photos of yourself and your family.

After you find the images, upload them or take screenshots. Resize them to fit your vision board. Attach 4-5 images to an email (or any other place that can grant you access to a printer) so they are not too big. Then, print them in color or black and white. This will help contribute to a vision board that reflects your goals.

### 3. **Visualize your goals:**

Close your eyes and imagine yourself already living your desired life. Visualize the details, emotions, and experiences associated with your goals. This step helps you connect with your desires on a deeper level. Imagine feet hitting the warm beach sands of Seychelles and experiencing the joy of manifesting your dream vacation before getting on a flight.

### 4. **Find visual representations:**

Look for images, words, and phrases in magazines or online that represent your goals and desires. Choose pictures that resonate with you and evoke positive emotions.

## 5. **Begin creating:**

Cut out your chosen images and words and arrange them on your poster board or cork board. Be creative and let your intuition guide you. You can also add personal photos, affirmations, or quotes that inspire you.

## 6. **Place your vision board where you can see it:**

Find a strategically visible place to display your vision board where you'll see it every day. It could be in your bedroom, office, or any other space that feels right for you.

## 7. **Visualize and feel your goals:**

Take a few minutes each day to look at your vision board and visualize yourself already living in the reality of your goals. Feel the emotions associated with achieving those goals. This practice helps to reinforce your intentions and keep you focused.

## 8. **Take inspired action:**

While visualization and positive thinking are important, taking action is crucial for manifesting your vision board. Break down your goals into actionable steps and start working towards them. Be open to opportunities and seize them when they arise.

## 9. **Start before you think you're ready:**

It is imperative not to postpone your journey toward your vision board's completion. The best time to start is now.

Instead of waiting for the perfect vision board, take action toward your goals and aspirations right away. By taking action now, you can sow the seed of success and begin the process of manifesting your aspirations. Even if your vision board is not yet finished, taking small steps and consistently making efforts can yield significant results over time. Therefore, it is paramount to seize the present moment and embark on your path to actualizing your dreams. Remember, progress and achievement lie in the journey, not just the destination.

Manifesting a vision board is a continuous process. Stay committed to your goals, believe in yourself, and trust the journey.

## Gathering Materials

To create a vision board, you'll need a variety of materials. These materials will serve as the foundation for your board and help bring your vision to life.

- **Choose a Base:** The base of your vision board can be anything that provides a sturdy surface for attaching images and quotes. A corkboard, poster board, or canvas can serve as an excellent base.

- **Choose a size** that suits your space and allows you to include all the elements of your vision without overcrowding. Consider whether you want your vision board to be portable or fixed in one location.

- **Collect and Curate Images:** Once you have your goals in mind, the next step is to curate images and quotes that represent those goals. This is where your creativity comes into play. Images are a crucial part of your vision board. They visually represent your goals and aspirations. Choose images that vividly represent your goals and evoke positive emotions. Magazines, printed photos, and online image sources like Pinterest can provide a wealth of imagery. Look for images that resonate with your vision. These could be pictures of dream destinations, successful people, or symbols of your goals. The more these images evoke positive emotions, the more effective they will be in inspiring you.

For example, if one of your goals is to travel to Paris, include images of the Eiffel Tower, French cafes, and Parisian streets. Select images that immediately resonate with you and reflect the essence of your goals. The more specific and detailed the images, the better they will serve as reminders of your aspirations.

- **Gather Quotes and Affirmations:** Quotes and affirmations add a powerful dimension to your vision board. They provide motivational messages and positive reinforcement.
Inspirational quotes from books, speeches, or personal mantras can be included. Choose quotes that speak to your heart, reflect the essence of your vision, and inspire and motivate you to pursue your goals. Quotes from successful individuals in your field or affirmations like "Believe in yourself and all that you are" can be powerful additions.

Look for quotes that not only inspire you but also align with your vision. Personalize them if needed to make them more relevant to your journey. Place these quotes prominently on your vision board where you can easily see and read them.
Similar to quotes, affirmations should be positive,

present-tense statements that reinforce your goals, such as "I am healthy and fit" or "I attract abundance and success."

- **Add Decorative Elements:** Decorative elements add a personal touch and make your vision board visually appealing.

  Stickers, washi tape, ribbons, and embellishments can enhance the aesthetic of your board. Use colors, patterns, and textures that you find inspiring and uplifting. The goal is to create a board that is not only meaningful but also a pleasure to look at.

- **Balance Visual and Text Elements:** Strike a balance between images and text to create a cohesive and visually appealing vision board.

  Arrange your board so that images and quotes complement each other rather than compete for attention.

  Consider the overall layout of your vision board. Group related images and quotes together to create sections or themes. This organization helps make your vision board more coherent and easier to focus on.

## Assemble Your Vision Board

With all your materials gathered and curated, it's time to assemble your vision board. This is where your vision tangibly comes to life.

- **Create a Layout:** Plan the layout of your vision board before attaching any items. This helps you visualize the final product and make adjustments as needed.

  You might arrange your board into sections for different areas of your life, such as health, career, and relationships.

  Lay out all your images, quotes, and decorative elements on the base without gluing them down. Experiment with different arrangements until you find one that feels right. Consider the flow and balance of your board, ensuring that it is visually pleasing and easy to navigate.

- **Attach Your Images and Quotes:** Securely attach your images and quotes to the base, using glue, tape, or pins.

  Use a glue stick for paper images, double-sided tape for heavier items, and push pins for a corkboard.

  Start attaching items from the center and work your way outwards. This helps ensure that everything fits and is properly aligned. Use different adhesive methods as needed to secure your items without damaging them.

- **Add Your Chosen Decorative Elements:** Enhance your vision board with decorative elements to make it more attractive and personalized.

Use washi tape to create borders, add stickers for visual interest, and incorporate ribbons or fabric for texture.

Personalize your vision board with elements that reflect your style and preferences. This not only makes the board more visually appealing but also more meaningful and enjoyable to look at.

- **Add Any Final Touches:** Review your vision board and make any final adjustments to ensure it aligns with your vision and goals.

  Step back and view your board as a whole, checking for balance, clarity, and completeness.

  Make sure every image and quote on your board serves a purpose and resonates with your goals. Adjust the layout if needed to create a harmonious and inspiring final product. Once you're satisfied, place your vision board in a prominent location where you can see it daily.

Creating a vision board is a deeply individualized, personal, and creative process that helps you connect with your goals and aspirations on a deeper level. By following these steps, you'll create a powerful visual tool that inspires and motivates you to achieve your dreams.

**Bringing it to Life:**

**My Vision Board Manifestation Experience**

While I guide you to create your vision board, I'd also like to provide some powerful personal examples of how vision boards have changed my life.

In creating my vision boards throughout the years, I've gathered images of things I wanted to manifest, such as attending the World Economic Forum in Davos, Switzerland. Finally, after seven years of focused visualization, I manifested that goal. I also included quotes and Bible verses to strengthen my faith and wrote down my desire to become an author on manifesting vision boards (and here I am!).

My vision board serves as a powerful tool that keeps me focused and reminds me of the impact I want my book to have on readers around the world.

Every time I look at my vision board, I feel a surge of motivation and determination to continue working on my manuscript. It serves as a constant reminder that my dream of becoming a published author is within reach.

Regularly engaging with your vision board, updating it as your dreams evolve, and sharing it with others for accountability can further enhance its effectiveness.

In conclusion, a vision board is a personalized and customizable tool that helps you clarify your vision, stay motivated, and take action toward your goals. It serves as a constant reminder of what you want to achieve and inspires you to make your dreams a reality. Unleash your creativity and create a vision board that will guide you on your journey toward success in any field you choose.

# CHAPTER SIX
# CATEGORIZING YOUR GOALS

The journey towards achieving success with your dream board begins with effectively characterizing your goals. Understanding the different types of goals—personal, professional, family, and group—can help create a balanced, comprehensive approach to creating the life of your dreams. Each category offers unique opportunities for growth and fulfillment.

## Personal Goals

Personal goals tend to focus on individual growth and overall well-being. These may include nurturing healthy relationships and prioritizing self-care.

For instance, making quality time for your spouse and intentionally carving out moments to connect with your children can foster deeper family bonds, creating a thriving family unit. Engaging in healthy activities, like going for walks or listening to your children's experiences, can strengthen these connections.

I discovered the importance of one-on-one time with my children when my 13-year-old daughter expressed a desire for individual outings rather than always being in a group. Her 11-year-old sister echoed this sentiment, revealing their wish to enjoy time alone with me. A memorable instance was when I took my 6-year-old daughter out for coffee; she insisted we sit down together, and her delighted exclamation, "Mama, are we having a girls' breakfast out? I enjoy our time together!" melted my heart. Such memories are vital for child development, helping to build their confidence.

Self-care is another crucial aspect that is often overlooked. In the hustle of caring for others, we frequently neglect our well-being. Setting health goals—like scheduling annual physicals, eating healthily, and exercising regularly—can significantly impact our lives. Simple pleasures, such as visiting a café alone once a week, can be incredibly rewarding.

It's important to be intentional about self-care. Self-care is not selfish; it's selfless. It's like the safety announcement or video on the plane before take-off; "if there is a sudden change in cabin pressure, pull sharply on the mask to start the flow
of oxygen, place the mask over your nose and mouth, and breathe normally before helping others. You need oxygen to help others get oxygen. Create a vision board with images or goals that inspire you. For example, I set a target to lose 60 pounds after gaining weight from having three children. This goal was motivated by a desire for better health. Through this process, I focused on my nutrition and even losing 20 pounds felt like an achievement. Each milestone celebrated reinforces a positive mindset, making the journey one of self-improvement.

Beyond health, personal development is another valuable focus. Reading, taking courses, or practicing new skills like communication or leadership fall under personal development. These goals enhance your abilities and equip you with tools to handle life's challenges with resilience.

## Professional Goals

Professional goals focus on your career aspirations, skill development, and advancement in your field. They could involve gaining new qualifications, advancing within your organization, or even transitioning into a new career path.

Consider someone re-entering the workforce after a long break—pursuing further education, like a master's or PhD, or completing certification courses can open new doors. For instance, an empty nester might seek to re-enter the workforce after a long absence by continuing their studies or transitioning into a new career path, such as becoming a teaching assistant and eventually a teacher.

Similarly, someone going through a divorce may choose to up-skill or pivot into new opportunities, especially if they were a stay-at-home parent and now need to provide for themselves. Setting objectives for career advancement, like aiming for a promotion or seeking leadership roles, becomes essential.

Acquiring new skills, particularly in emerging technologies, is vital in today's job market. Certifications, such as HR accreditations or attending workshops, can enhance expertise and open new opportunities. Joining organizations like the New York Africa Chamber of Commerce or local chambers can also provide networking opportunities.

Setting goals for career advancement—such as securing a promotion or joining a leadership program—helps keep you motivated and progressing. I'm presently manifesting a career development goal as an MBA student. If you want to earn more, learn more. Growth in relevant knowledge typically increases your value to employers and clients.

## Group Goals

Group goals involve collective objectives that require collaboration within teams, organizations, or communities. These goals emphasize teamwork and shared accountability.

For example, during the summer, I participated in a work-study project for the city of Newark, working with about 300 students aged 14 to 19. I conducted vision board workshops and developed the curriculum for them. Witnessing the benefits to the students was rewarding, and I learned to adjust my approach to different settings, including understanding what motivates teenagers. Not every student aspires to go to college; some may find fulfilling careers in trade schools, such as becoming electricians or construction workers.

I also facilitated a workshop for a college readiness program involving teenage girls for the YWCA of New York. I discovered that many thought they had aged out of volunteerism since they were left with only one year to graduate. However, upon speaking to the program coordinator we realized that their two-year commitment to the program counts as volunteerism and would enhance their college applications, showing how vision boarding can aid in team development and provide invaluable support.

Fostering a positive team environment through team-building activities improves collaboration. I found that vision board events are similar to board games, encouraging competition and camaraderie. The laughter and creativity involved in cutting out images and using glue sticks help build confidence and strengthen relationships.

# Chapter Seven
# MANIFEST YOUR DREAM

The journey to creating the life of your dreams begins with taking the first step. Don't be intimidated—don't let fear hold you back! The courage to take the first step in creating your vision board is commendable, and you deserve applause for it!

Many people, especially those from cultures that emphasize risk avoidance, grapple with questions like, "Am I doing the right thing?" or "Am I good enough?" I understand this struggle firsthand. Moving to the United States of America taught me to see failure as a stepping stone to success, and that embracing resilience helps us grow, fosters new connections, and opens doors to exciting opportunities.

Creating vision boards is a unique journey where bonds are formed, friendships flourish, businesses take off, and lives transform. Envisioning your dreams is simply manifesting the power of endless possibilities.

## The Process of Manifesting Your Vision

The process of manifesting your vision involves setting a clear intention, visualizing your goals, taking inspired action, and maintaining a positive mindset. To manifest your vision accurately, there are very important steps you must take so that you don't go in circles wasting time, and delaying yourself. Below are crucial steps to guide you.

65

- **Set a Clear Intention:** Start by defining what you want to achieve. Be specific about your goals and the outcomes you desire.

  Instead of saying "I want to be successful," specify what success looks like to you—perhaps "I want to build a successful online business that generates a steady income."

  Clarity is key to manifestation. The more specific your intention, the easier it is to visualize and work towards it. Ambiguous goals lack direction and are harder to achieve.

- **Visualize Your Goals:** Regularly visualize your goals as if they have already been achieved. Use all your senses to create a vivid mental image.

  If your goal is to own a home, visualize every detail of the house, from the color of the walls to the layout of the garden. Visualization helps bridge the gap between your current reality and your desired future. It creates a mental blueprint that guides your actions and decisions.

- **Take Inspired Action:** Visualization alone is not enough; you must take concrete steps toward your goals. Break down your vision into actionable steps and start working on them.

  If your vision is to write a book, set a daily writing goal, outline your chapters, and seek feedback from peers. Action is the bridge between dreams and reality. Even small, consistent actions can lead to significant progress over time. Never forget that without action, this is you simply building castles in the sky. Actions are the wings your dreams use to fly

*"Actions are the wings your dreams use to fly"* - **Busie Matsiko**

- **Maintain a Positive Mindset:** Stay positive and believe in your ability to achieve your vision. Overcome self-doubt and negative thoughts by focusing on your strengths and past successes.

  Silence the voice of past failure by reminding yourself of the challenges you overcame in the past and using that confidence to tackle current obstacles. A positive mindset is crucial for overcoming challenges and staying motivated. It helps you maintain resilience and perseverance in the face of setbacks.

**Key Questions to ASK as you continue to MANIFEST your vision board: Why, When, and How?**

To effectively manifest your vision, ask yourself these key questions:

## Why?

Understand the deeper reasons behind your goals. Why do you want to achieve this vision? What will it bring to your life? For instance, if your vision is to travel the world, your "why" might be to experience different cultures and gain new perspectives. Knowing your "why" provides motivation and clarity, connecting your vision to your core values and desires. Knowing your "why" keeps you going against all odds.

## When?

Set a timeline for your goals. When do you want to achieve them? Deadlines create a sense of urgency and help you stay on track. For example, if your vision is to complete a marathon, choose a specific race date and plan your training schedule accordingly. Deadlines transform your vision into tangible goals, prioritizing your actions and maintaining focus.

## How?

Develop a clear plan of action. How will you achieve your vision? What steps do you need to take? If your vision is to launch a business, outline steps such as market research, creating a business plan, securing funding, and marketing your product. A detailed plan provides a roadmap for achieving your vision, breaking larger goals into manageable tasks.

If you don't know how to accomplish something on your dream board; it doesn't mean you should remove it. It means you set a goal to learn how to accomplish it.

By answering these questions before you embark on your vision board journey, you create a solid foundation for your vision and a clear roadmap to follow. This structured approach ensures you stay focused, motivated, and on track toward achieving your desired future.

## Manifesting Your Vision: The Process

Manifesting your vision is a multi-faceted endeavor involving mental, emotional, and physical elements. It's about defining your deepest desires, visualizing them vividly, and taking deliberate steps to bring them into reality. Manifestation is not wishful thinking; it requires a proactive approach to align your internal mindset with your external actions.

**Define Your Vision:** Your vision is a detailed image of your ideal future, encompassing personal, professional, and spiritual goals. Ask yourself what truly excites you. What kind of life do you want to lead? Define your vision in detail, considering all aspects of your life, including career, relationships, health, and personal growth.

**Visualize Success:** Visualization involves creating a mental image of your desired outcome with as much detail and emotion as possible. Use all your senses to make your visualization vivid and real. How often should you practice this? As often as it comes to mind until it's engraved in your subconscious.

## The Principles of Vision Board Manifestation

The principles for manifesting your vision board are rooted in the law of attraction and the power of visualization. The law of attraction suggests that your thoughts shape your reality. Here are the core principles:

**1. Clarity:** A vision board helps you gain clarity about your goals by defining your desires, and setting clear intentions to guide your thoughts and actions.

**2. Visualization:** Visualizing yourself living your desired life activates your imagination and emotions, aligning your subconscious with your conscious intentions.

**3. Positive Emotions:** The images and words on your vision board should evoke joy, excitement, and gratitude, increasing your vibrational energy and attracting those experiences.

**4. Focus:** Your vision board serves as a visual representation of your goals. Regularly focusing on it keeps your attention aligned with what you want to manifest.

**5. Belief:** Believing in the possibility of your dreams is fundamental. Faith in yourself and the process fosters a positive mindset.

**6. Action:** While visualization is important, taking action is crucial. Your vision board guides you in identifying necessary steps, creating momentum toward realizing your dreams.

Remember, the principles of a vision board are tools to focus your thoughts, emotions, and actions toward manifesting your goals. They empower you to take the necessary steps to achieve your vision.

*"Manifesting my vision board allowed me to tease out of my mind my half-formed thoughts, my half-formed dreams, and clarify my intent and my objectives. Sitting with like-minded people who had similar dreams and objectives, like similar branches of the same tree, helped to focus the year ahead with intent. Anything you achieve starts with intent."*

— **Sophia Jingo**, *Chief Auditor, Citi Internal Audit*

With these insights and strategies, you're equipped to start your journey of manifesting your vision. Embrace the process, celebrate your successes, and remember—your future is filled with limitless potential!

*"I used to be skeptical about vision boards because many in my Christian community believed vision boards were about manifesting things outside of God's will, relying on personal power rather than divine guidance. However, as I studied God's word, I realized that Scripture encourages us to write our vision. We, as His children, have the opportunity to partner with Him and manifest His plans for our lives through His power. With this new perspective, building vision boards grounded in God's word has become a powerful experience. I've witnessed goals, visions, and dreams come to life by writing them down and making them clear for all to see. This practice has led to moments of praising our Heavenly Father for His faithfulness and guidance."*

**Stephanie Lamour,** *Christian Counselor & Coach*

## Chapter Eight
# DIGITAL VS. PHYSICAL VISION BOARDS

Creating a vision board is a powerful exercise in visualizing dreams, setting goals, and manifesting intentions.

Your choice of using a physical or digital vision board is now easier with the ever-growing integration of technology into our lives, the way we approach this exercise has also evolved.

Vision boards are no longer confined to the walls of our rooms or corkboards at our desks. They can now be created digitally, accessible from virtually any device, anywhere. But which medium should you choose?

You can take your vision board with you, everywhere you go and be inspired on the move. In this chapter, we'll explore the differences between digital and physical vision boards, the benefits of each, and tips to help you select the medium that best aligns with your lifestyle, preferences, and goals.

**The Power of Vision Boards**

Before diving into the specifics of digital and physical vision boards, it's important to reiterate why vision boards are so effective. Vision boards are a blend of goal-setting, visualization, and positive reinforcement. They provide a tangible (or digital) reminder of what you aspire to achieve, whether those goals are personal, professional, or both.

When you look at a vision board regularly, it reinforces your commitment to your goals, helping you stay motivated and focused.

Studies have shown that visualization can enhance motivation, improve performance, and boost confidence. Creating and engaging with images, words, and other visuals that represent our dreams, inspires our minds to work toward them. A vision board helps turn abstract goals into visual representations, making them feel more attainable. The key is choosing a format that feels inspiring and accessible to you.

## Digital Vision Boards

In today's digital age, the concept of a vision board has expanded to include various online and app-based platforms. With countless apps, websites, and digital tools available, creating a digital vision board can be as simple as dragging and dropping images onto a virtual canvas.

## Benefits of Digital Vision Boards

1.  **Accessibility**: One of the biggest advantages of a digital vision board is that it can go wherever you go. Whether on your phone, tablet, or laptop, you can easily access your vision board anytime you need a boost of motivation.

2.  **Unlimited Customization**: Digital tools allow for limitless design options. You can add photos, text, videos, and even audio clips. Many apps provide built-in resources, such as image libraries and design

templates, to make creating a vision board easy and visually appealing.

3. **Eco-Friendly**: A digital vision board eliminates the need for physical materials, reducing waste. For those conscious of environmental impact, this option can be both a creative and sustainable choice.

4. **Flexibility**: Digital vision boards are easily editable. You can update or rearrange items as your goals evolve, without the need to start over or worry about damaging physical materials.

5. **Increased Security and Privacy**: If you're using a private app or platform, your vision board remains personal and secure, allowing you to reflect on your goals without needing to display them publicly.

## Popular Digital Vision Board Platforms

Some popular platforms for creating digital vision boards include:

- **Pinterest**: Known for its vast library of images, Pinterest is a go-to platform for curating a vision board. You can create private boards and pin images, quotes, and ideas that resonate with your goals.

- **Canva**: With its drag-and-drop features and design tools, Canva allows for easy creation of custom vision boards. You can incorporate photos, text, and

CREATE THE LIFE OF YOUR DREAMS

graphics for a professional-looking board. There's a
free version available.

- **Milanote**: This tool is ideal for creative minds,
  offering a blank canvas to organize ideas, goals, and
  visuals in any format you like. It's highly customizable
  and intuitive.

- **Vision Board Apps**: Apps such as "Hay House
  Vision Board," "Visuapp," and "MindMovies" are
  designed specifically for digital vision boards, often
  with additional tools for tracking progress,
  affirmations, and more.

## Physical Vision Boards

Physical vision boards are another create and popular choice
because of their tactile nature and the tangible connection
they provide. Creating a physical vision board involves
selecting magazine clippings, photos, quotes, and other
materials to paste onto a board or canvas. For some, this
hands-on experience enhances the emotional connection to
their goals.

## Benefits of Physical Vision Boards

1. **Sensory Experience**: Physically creating a vision
   board is a tactile process that can help solidify your
   commitment to your goals. Cutting out images,
   arranging them, and gluing them down engages the
   senses and may make the experience feel more
   immersive and memorable.

2.  **Visual Impact**: Physical vision boards are often displayed in a visible area of your home or workspace. Seeing it daily serves as a consistent reminder of your goals and intentions.

3.  **Creativity and Personalization**: There's something deeply personal about selecting physical items to represent your aspirations. The process of choosing and arranging materials can feel like a form of meditation, allowing you to reflect on your goals more deeply.

4.  **Symbolic Value**: The tangible nature of a physical vision board can make it feel more "real." For some, having a physical reminder on display helps create a sense of accountability and emotional connection to their goals.

## Tips for Creating a Physical Vision Board

To create a meaningful physical vision board, consider the following tips:

-   **Gather a Variety of Materials**: Collect magazines, printed photos, fabric swatches, and any other items that resonate with your goals. You might even incorporate small objects, like a keychain from a dream destination or a dried flower representing growth.

- **Choose a Dedicated Space**: Decide on a size and place that suits your lifestyle. This could be a large board on the wall, a small framed board on your desk, or even a scrapbook that you can keep private.

- **Take Your Time**: Unlike digital boards, physical boards are harder to change once completed. Take your time arranging items and deciding on the final layout to ensure it accurately represents your vision.

## How to Choose Your Vision Board Medium

Now that we've explored both digital and physical options, let's look at some questions to help you decide which medium best suits you:

1. **What is Your Lifestyle Like?**: If you're always on the go or don't have a specific space for a physical board, a digital vision board may be more practical. If you spend a lot of time at home or have a dedicated workspace, a physical board might fit right into your environment.

2. **How Often Do You Want to Update It?**: If you envision frequently changing or adding to your board, a digital platform allows for easy modifications. If you prefer a more fixed display, a physical board might suit your needs better.

3. **What Type of Experience Do You Prefer?**: If you enjoy hands-on creative projects, a physical board offers a tactile and meditative process. On the other

hand, if you appreciate streamlined, digital designs, you may enjoy the simplicity and versatility of a digital board.

4.  **Do You Prefer Privacy or Public Inspiration?**: For those who prefer to keep their goals private, a digital board can be stored discreetly on a device. However, if you're inspired by sharing or seeing your vision daily, a physical board displayed in your space might feel more impactful.

5.  **How Much Time Can You Dedicate?**: Physical boards may require more time to gather materials, assemble, and complete. Digital boards, especially if you're using pre-existing images, can be quicker to set up.

## Combining Digital and Physical Elements

It's worth noting that some people enjoy combining both mediums. For instance, you might create a digital board for portability and accessibility while maintaining a smaller physical version for personal inspiration. Or you might use digital images to print and paste onto a physical board, blending both experiences. You might even create a physical board; take a picture of it for your phone or to be used as a screensaver on your computer.

## Conclusion: Find What Resonates with You

Ultimately, the choice between a digital and physical vision board is a personal one. Both mediums offer unique advantages, and neither is inherently better than the other. What matters most is that the vision board resonates with you inspire you and fit into your lifestyle in a meaningful way. Whether you're flipping through a beautifully crafted Pinterest board on your phone or glancing at a colorful board on your wall, let it be a reminder that you are intentionally manifesting the life of your dreams.

## Chapter Nine
# PRETTY PICTURES BECOME POWERFUL PLANS

A vision board is a beautiful, inspiring display of your goals and dreams, but what transforms those "pretty pictures" into reality is an actionable plan.

A well-constructed vision board is a powerful tool to clarify your intentions, spark motivation, and give you a visual reminder of your desired goals. However, to fully realize its potential, your vision board needs a roadmap—one that translates inspiration into tangible steps.

In this chapter, we'll explore the process of building an action roadmap for your vision board, breaking down dreams into achievable milestones and daily habits. By the end, you'll be able to turn the inspiring images and affirmations on your vision board into a clear, structured path forward.

### Why You Need an Action Roadmap

Creating a vision board allows you to visualize your dreams, but without a strategy, it can be easy to lose sight of how to achieve them. An action roadmap bridges the gap between where you are now and where you desire to go by breaking down your goals into smaller, more manageable steps.

This roadmap turns your vision board from a source of passive inspiration into a practical guide, helping you stay focused, track progress, and adjust as needed. A roadmap also serves as a way to keep yourself accountable, ensuring that your vision board doesn't just stay on the wall or screen, but actively drives you toward your goals. The Vision Board is where you desire to go, your action roadmap takes you there.

## Step 1: Clarify Your Goals and Prioritize

Start by taking a closer look at your vision board. Identify the specific goals or themes that stand out. Are you aiming for career advancement, personal growth, health, travel, or financial success? Write down the core areas represented on your vision board. Then, prioritize these goals. Which ones are most important to you right now? Which will have the biggest impact on your life?

Prioritization helps you focus on what matters most. If everything is equally important; nothing is important. While your board may represent a wide array of dreams, it's essential to determine which goals you'll tackle first. Begin with one or two key areas, then add additional goals as you make progress. Your first one can be the most rewarding or the easiest to accomplish that way.

### Exercise: Goal Reflection
1. Take a few minutes to reflect on each image, quote, or symbol on your vision board.
2. Write down the goal or aspiration each element represents.
3. Rank these goals in terms of importance or the level of impact they would have on your life.

## Step 2: Break Down Big Goals into Smaller Milestones

Once you've prioritized your main goals, the next step is to break each one down into smaller, actionable milestones.

Major goals can feel overwhelming if viewed as a single task, but by dividing them into smaller steps, you create a clear and manageable path to success.

For example, if your vision board has an image representing financial independence, you could break this down into steps like creating a budget, paying off debt, building an emergency fund, and then focusing on investments or passive income streams. Each of these steps could be broken down further into monthly or weekly goals.

## Exercise: Milestone Mapping

1. Choose one priority goal from your vision board.
2. Think of 3-5 major milestones that would signify progress toward this goal.
3. Break down each milestone into smaller, actionable steps.
4. List these steps in a sequence or timeline, making it easy to track and follow.

## Step 3: Set SMART Goals

To make your roadmap effective, set SMART (Specific, Measurable, Achievable, Relevant, Time-bound) goals for each milestone. SMART goals transform vague aspirations into concrete plans.

For instance, if one of your vision board goals is "Get Fit," a SMART goal would be "Complete a 5K run within six months by running three times a week." This version is specific (complete a 5K), measurable (track distance and time), achievable (consistent training), relevant (supports your health goal), and time-bound (within six months).

## SMART Goal Examples

- **Career Advancement**: "Complete a certification course in my field within the next three months, dedicating two hours every weekend."

- **Health**: "Increase my water intake to eight glasses a day by setting reminders on my phone."

- **Finances**: "Save $1,000 in an emergency fund within four months by setting aside $250 per month."

By setting SMART goals, you create clarity and structure for each item on your vision board, helping you maintain motivation and recognize progress.

## Step 4: Create a Timeline and Schedule Check-ins

With milestones and SMART goals in place, establish a timeline. Assign specific timeframes to each milestone and mark regular check-ins to review your progress. Setting a timeline helps you stay accountable and gives you a sense of momentum. For some goals, weekly check-ins may be ideal; for others, monthly reviews may be more appropriate.

Use a planner, calendar app, or goal-tracking tool to set reminders for each milestone. Regular check-ins are also an opportunity to celebrate small wins, reevaluate steps, and make adjustments if necessary.

**Suggested Timeline Structure**

- **Weekly Goals**: Track small tasks or habits (e.g., exercising, saving money, journaling).

- **Monthly Goals**: Review milestone progress (e.g., paying down debt, taking a course module).

- **Quarterly Goals**: Reflect on major milestones, make adjustments, and set the next quarter's priorities.

**Step 5: Develop Daily Habits That Support Your Vision**

To stay aligned with your vision board, establish daily habits that reflect the goals you want to achieve. If your board includes a goal to improve mental health, incorporate meditation, journaling, or gratitude practices into your daily routine. If you're focusing on career growth, dedicate a few minutes each day to learning a new skill, networking, or updating your resume.

Daily habits are powerful because they compound over time, turning small actions into significant progress.

**Example Daily Habits**
- **Career Growth**: Spend 10 minutes each morning reading industry news.

- **Health**: Walk for 30 minutes each day.

- **Mindset**: Start each day with an affirmation aligned with your vision board.

## Step 6: Track Your Progress and Celebrate Wins

Tracking your progress keeps you motivated and helps you recognize how far you've come. Create a progress tracker that outlines each milestone and check it regularly. Celebrate small wins along the way, as they reinforce your commitment and provide a confidence boost.

Whether it's a journal, spreadsheet, or a dedicated app, tracking your progress shows you the connection between daily actions and long-term achievements. Celebrating wins —big or small—keeps your journey positive and reminds you that every step forward matters.

### Exercise: Progress Journal

1. Create a journal entry for each milestone or goal.

2. Record the actions you've taken, any challenges, and how you feel about your progress.

3. Write down any adjustments you plan to make, and celebrate each step forward.

## Step 7: Revisit and Refresh Your Vision Board

As you make progress, it's natural for your goals to evolve. Revisit your vision board periodically and refresh it as needed. Perhaps you've achieved some goals and want to add new aspirations, or maybe your priorities have shifted. Updating your vision board keeps it aligned with your current path and ensures it continues to inspire you.

If you're using a digital vision board, this might be as simple as adding new images or rearranging old ones. For a physical board, consider replacing or layering new visuals. A refreshed vision board reflects your growth and reaffirms your commitment to your journey.

**Bringing It All Together: Your Vision Board Action Roadmap**

1. **Prioritize Goals**: Identify and rank the core goals on your vision board.

2. **Break Down Milestones**: Divide each major goal into smaller, achievable milestones.

3. **Set SMART Goals**: Define each milestone with clear, actionable SMART goals.

4. **Establish a Timeline**: Assign timelines to your goals and set check-in dates.

5. **Develop Daily Habits**: Create daily routines that align with your vision.

6.  **Track Progress and Celebrate Wins**: Document your progress and recognize achievements.

7.  **Revisit and Refresh**: Update your vision board as you grow and achieve.

# Chapter Ten
# SETTING TIMELINES

*"People overestimate what they can do in a year and underestimate what they can do in two or three decades."-* **Tony Robbins**

Vision boards are powerful tools for visualizing and manifesting our goals.

However, to turn dreams into reality, it's crucial to incorporate timelines into the process. Timelines bring structure, urgency, and purpose, empowering you to not only envision your aspirations but to actively pursue and achieve them.

As Tony Robbins wisely notes, *"People overestimate what they can do in a year and underestimate what they can do in two or three decades."* With clearly defined, realistic timelines, you're better equipped to navigate the journey toward your vision, focusing on both the immediate steps and the milestones along the way.

## The Importance of Timelines in Vision Boards

Setting a realistic timeline provides you with a roadmap for achieving your goals. It clarifies the steps you need to take and helps maintain focus, motivation, and accountability. When you know what you're working toward and when you hope to reach it, each milestone becomes a reminder of the progress you're making.

Timelines help articulate your endurance level, resilience, and commitment. Just as a student knows when graduation is expected or an employee works toward an annual review, having a timeline keeps you disciplined and focused, helping you avoid distractions.

## Suggested Timeline Milestones

When setting timelines for your vision board, it can be helpful to divide your journey into incremental milestones, such as 30 days, three months, six months, and one year. Each interval serves as a checkpoint where you can assess your progress, recalibrate if necessary, and celebrate your achievements. Here's how you can structure these timelines:

## 30 Days: Building Momentum

The first 30 days are all about taking initial steps and building momentum. This is the time to set immediate goals and identify "quick wins" that will give you a boost of motivation. For example, you might:

- Purchase a book related to your goal, take a short course, or make a small but meaningful change in your routine.

- Create a daily affirmation practice that keeps your vision at the forefront of your mind.

- Establish a routine that aligns with your goals, such as working out, meditating, or starting the day with a gratitude list.

These tasks may require minimal resources but can yield significant satisfaction, setting the tone for continued action. Consistent small actions over the first month will build confidence and lay a strong foundation for your journey.

## Three Months: Reassessing and Strengthening

At the three-month mark, take time to reflect on your progress and reassess your goals. This period is about engaging more deeply with your vision, evaluating how far you've come, and adjusting your path if necessary. Consider:

· Setting immediate, action-oriented goals based on your vision, such as completing a relevant course, reaching out to potential mentors, or starting a side project.

· Acknowledging and celebrating small victories, as recognition fuels further motivation and marks your progress toward larger goals.

· Reaffirming your commitment with daily or weekly reflections on your achievements and challenges.

Three months is also a great time to start turning your "vision board" into a "doing board." Use a journal or planner to track your incremental goals and actions, complementing the macro view provided by your vision board.

## Six Months: Reflection and Recalibration

Six months is often a pivotal point on your vision board journey. By now, you'll have made significant strides, and this is an ideal time for a deeper reflection on both accomplishments and setbacks. Evaluate whether your vision still resonates, and be open to recalibration:

· Revisit your vision board and adjust elements that may need tweaking based on your experiences.

· Consider areas for personal development, like taking a public speaking course or honing time management skills.

· Invest in refining any necessary skills, whether technical, interpersonal, or otherwise, that will help you continue progressing toward your larger vision.

During this stage, your vision board acts as a touchstone, a reminder of the progress you've made, and an anchor for any course adjustments.

## One Year: Reflecting and Planning Ahead
The one-year mark is not only about reviewing your accomplishments but also about preparing for the future. At this point, evaluate what you've achieved, what you've learned, and where you want to go next. This stage might involve:

· Conducting a full review of your vision board and the goals you set.

· Setting new visions or recalibrating your goals for the upcoming year, perhaps dreaming even bigger.

· Reconsidering any goals that may not have been feasible this year and brainstorming ways to accomplish those next year.

Incorporating these timelines into your vision board journey provides the structure to keep moving forward. Remember, every step, no matter how small, brings you closer to your vision. With patience, persistence, and a clear path, your vision is within reach. Keep dreaming big and take consistent action—you've got this!

## Chapter Eleven
# FROM MY HEART TO YOURS

*"It always seems impossible until it's done." -* **Nelson Mandela**

As we come to the end of this book; I want to leave you with some final thoughts from my heart to yours. Creating the life of your dreams can be immensely rewarding, yet it's not without its challenges. To truly harness the power of your vision board, it's essential to tackle procrastination, manage disorganization, address doubts and fears, learn to fail forward, stay motivated, and effectively deal with setbacks. This note provides personally tested strategies for overcoming these common obstacles.

## FALLING OFF THE BANDWAGON

If you find yourself falling off the bandwagon and becoming inconsistent in the pursuit of your goal; don't beat yourself down, pick yourself up, retrace your steps to identify where and why you missed, adjust where necessary, and start over.

## FAILING FORWARD

Failure is not final. No matter how hard we prepare for a journey; sometimes; failure is inevitable. You don't have to stop dreaming because you failed in your attempt to achieve a goal. Just like an actor doesn't stop acting because they missed a line. The Director shouts "Cut" and they do another "Take". When you experience failure your journey to success; shout "CUT" and do another "TAKE". In your second take;

93

you are armed with the wisdom of not repeating what you missed in your first take.

## WHEN THE VISION IS NOT WORKING

"You've got to know when to hold 'em
Know when to fold 'em
Know when to walk away
And know when to run...." A line from Kenny Roger's Song; The Gambler.

A friend of mine and her husband had hoped for a baby boy for years, as they already had two beautiful girls. They put this wish on their vision board and bought baby boy clothes, believing this would help manifest their dream. However, they later discovered they were pregnant with another baby girl. At that moment, they realized they had done their best to make their dream come true, but it was no longer realistic. They found a family to donate the boy's clothes to, and happily prepared for the arrival of their daughter. The journey to creating the life of your dreams demands your best, and after you've given your best over and over without accomplishing it. It might simply mean the timing of that vision isn't right, and you have to heed the wisdom of Kenny Roger's song referenced earlier: "Know when to talk away..." walking away isn't giving up, it's recognizing that every seed grows beautifully in its time. When the vision is in its right time, struggle is minimized, and success is inevitable.

## Dealing with Procrastination and Disorganization

If you struggle with procrastination or disorganization, vision boarding can be a game-changer. Many people have multiple to-do lists scattered across notebooks, sticky notes, or agendas, with tasks that often go unfinished. Maybe you set out to work on a project or achieve a goal, but life gets in the way, and your plans fall by the wayside. Or perhaps you've started several journals, only to forget about them over time. Vision boarding creates a centralized, visual reminder of your goals, offering a structured way to organize your ambitions and stay focused.

A vision board serves as a "big picture" document, visually representing what you aim to achieve. Placing it in a prominent space—whether in your bedroom, study, or workspace—keeps your goals front and center, acting as a reminder to stay on track. When you see images of what you've set out to do each day, it reinforces your commitment and can nudge you back on course if you veer off.

This practice has personally helped me overcome procrastination. I used to rely on "Post-its and scattered notes" but often felt frustrated when I didn't complete my tasks. Vision boarding has not only improved my organization but also acts as a prompt to catch up on things I might otherwise forget. By sharing ideas with others who face similar challenges, I've realized I'm not alone in these struggles. For example, some people have strengths in areas where I might need help, and that's okay. I've learned to delegate tasks to those who excel in them, embracing vulnerability as a strength. Recognizing where you need support is essential because you can't get help if you're not open to it.

Vision boarding won't solve every issue, but it will alleviate frustration, disappointment, and disorganization—and sometimes even reduce these obstacles altogether.

## Confronting Doubts and Fears

Doubts and fears remind us of our humanity but shouldn't hinder guys from achieving extraordinary goals. Confronting your doubts and fears from the beginning of the journey is another critical step in overcoming challenges.

These emotions are natural and often stem from past experiences or fear of the unknown. Begin by acknowledging your doubts without judgment, and challenge them by reframing them positively.

For example, if you doubt your ability to achieve a goal, remind yourself of past successes and embrace your existing skills. Visualization and affirmations can be powerful here; use your vision board to reinforce positive beliefs and imagine yourself achieving your goals.

Surround yourself with supportive people who encourage you. Facing doubts head-on builds resilience and fosters a positive mindset.

## Staying Motivated

Motivation is crucial for maintaining momentum with your vision board goals. Motivation can fade over time, especially if progress is slow or obstacles arise. Set clear, achievable milestones to keep you focused and remind yourself why these goals matter. Regularly revisit your vision board, incorporating motivational quotes and images that inspire you. Celebrating small victories boosts confidence and reinforces your commitment.

Establishing a routine with daily or weekly check-ins helps maintain focus and enthusiasm. Seek inspiration from books, podcasts, or mentors who share your goals. By actively cultivating motivation, you keep the energy and drive to work toward your vision.

## Dealing with Setbacks

Setbacks are inevitable on any journey toward significant goals, but they offer valuable learning opportunities. When faced with a setback, take a step back to assess it objectively. Identify the factors involved and consider any necessary adjustments. Reflect on your vision board to see if goals or strategies need revision. Staying flexible is key; understand that setbacks don't define your journey—they're part of it. Develop a plan to overcome each setback with manageable steps, and consider seeking insights from mentors, friends, or a coach.

Self-compassion is essential; avoid harsh self-criticism and acknowledge your efforts. Setbacks are temporary, and with patience and persistence, you can overcome them.

## Conclusion: From Vision to Reality

Creating an action roadmap transforms your vision board from a beautiful collage into a strategic guide. This process doesn't require perfection but rather consistency, commitment, and a willingness to adapt. With your action roadmap in hand, you now have the tools to make the life of your dreams a reality, one step at a time. Let your vision board be the spark, and let your roadmap be the path. Embrace each step forward, knowing that you're actively creating the future you envision.

I look forward to hearing your story as you embark on this amazing journey to create the life of your dreams!

www.ingramcontent.com/pod-product-compliance
Lightning Source LLC
Chambersburg PA
CBHW061705120626
46550CB00003B/1100